MW01152096

THE STORY OF THE

KANSAS CITY CHIEFS

By Mark and Solomon Shulman

Kaleidoscope
Minneapolis, MN

BIGFOOT BOOKS

The Quest for Discovery Never Ends

....

This edition first published in 2021 by Kaleidoscope Publishing, Inc.

No part of this publication may be reproduced in whole or in part without written permission of the publisher.

For information regarding permission, write to Kaleidoscope Publishing, Inc. 6012 Blue Circle Drive Minnetonka, MN 55343

Library of Congress Control Number 2020933957

ISBN 978-1-64519-233-6 (library bound) 978-1-64519-301-2 (ebook)

Printed in the United States of America.

FIND ME IF YOU CAN!

Bigfoot lurks within one of the images in this book. It's up to you to find him!

TABLE OF
CONTENTS

KICKOFF!

What's red and white and loud all over? The mighty Chiefs fans! When the game begins, KC fans scream and chop the air. Their team has been tough and brave for years. The Chiefs played in the very first Super Bowl. And they're one of the best teams in today's NFL. They gave their fans a big reason to cheer in 2020. The Chiefs won Super Bowl LIV!

Will they give their famous fans more to cheer for?

The Super Bowl parade ended with a rally at city hall in Kansas City.

In 1960, the American Football League (AFL) started. One AFL team was the Dallas Texans. The Texans were owned by Lamar Hunt. He also started basketball, hockey, and soccer teams.

The Texans won the 1962 AFL Championship. They defeated the Houston Oilers.

In 1963, the Texans moved to Kansas City and changed their name. They became the Kansas City Chiefs. The AFL then joined the NFL. Starting in 1966, there would be a new championship game. The Chiefs played in the very first Super Bowl. They lost to the NFL's Green Bay Packers.

Three years later, the Chiefs went back. This time, they won the Super Bowl!

FUN FACT

The first two Super Bowls were, at first, named the AFL-NFL World Championship Game.

Celebration! The Texans had fun after winning the 1962 AFL title.

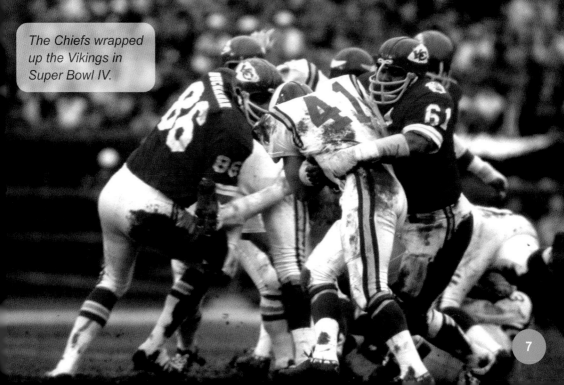

The Chiefs wrapped up the Vikings in Super Bowl IV.

After winning Super Bowl IV, the Chiefs struggled. They reached the playoffs twice in 20 seasons. Fans kept filling Arrowhead Stadium. They cheered no matter what!

Things looked up in 1989. Coach Marty Schottenheimer put together a winning team. He used the **West Coast Offense** to pass the ball more. Two Hall of Famers helped the team win. Quarterback Joe Montana ran the offense. Marcus Allen ran the ball. The Chiefs went to the playoffs seven times from 1990 to 1997.

Lamar Hunt named the Super Bowl. He was inspired by these kids' toys called Super Balls!

Joe Montana

Alex Smith

The Chiefs had some good teams in the early
2000s. None made it far in the playoffs, however. In
2013, Alex Smith became the next big Chiefs passing
star. In his first year, the Chiefs started 9–0. Their
strong passing game was a big threat in the AFC
West. Smith and Kansas City won their division in
2016 and 2017.

During the 2017 season, Smith sat out one game. A **rookie** took the field. His name was Patrick Mahomes. The rest is Chiefs history.

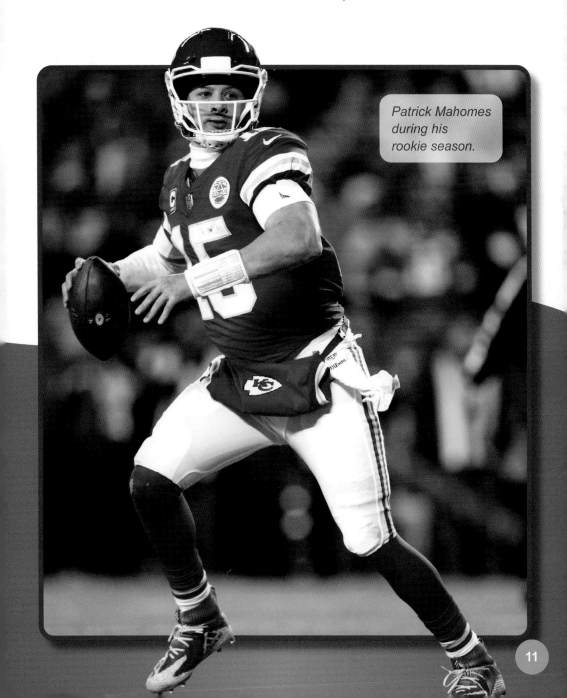

Patrick Mahomes during his rookie season.

Mahomes became **starting** QB in 2018. His skills thrilled Chiefs fans. He set a team record with 50 TD passes. Mahomes connected with Tyreek Hill and Travis Kelce over and over. The Chiefs finished 12–4. That was the best record in the AFC. The Chiefs went all the way to the AFC Championship Game.

In 2019, they got even better! Mahomes was a star again. The defense got better. The team went 12-4 again. They beat the Titans in the AFC Championship Game. In Super Bowl LIV, Kansas City beat the 49ers. Mahomes and the Chiefs were champs!

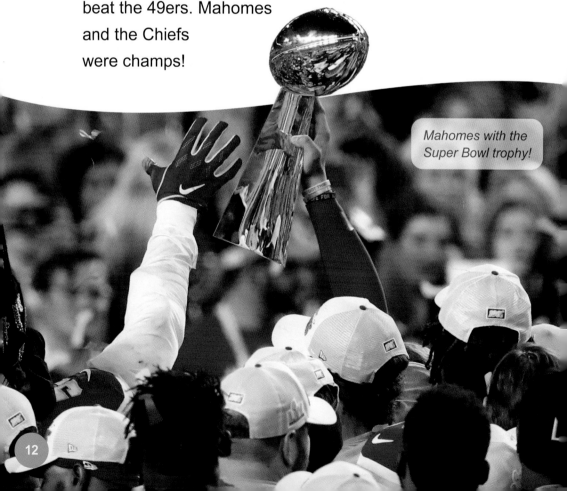

Mahomes with the Super Bowl trophy!

TIMELINE OF THE KANSAS CITY CHIEFS

1960

1960:
The Dallas Texans join the new AFL.

1963

1963:
The Texans become the Kansas City Chiefs.

1966

1966:
Chiefs play in the first Super Bowl.

1969

1969:
Chiefs win Super Bowl IV.

1986

1986:
Chiefs return to the playoffs for the first time in 15 years.

2018

2018:
Chiefs reach the AFC Championship Game.

2019

2019:
Chiefs win Super Bowl LIV. They beat San Francisco 31–20.

CHAMPIONS AGAIN!

Tyreek Hill caught the biggest pass of the Super Bowl!

In 1970, the Chiefs won Super Bowl IV. Then their fans waited fifty years for another chance. K.C. reached Super Bowl LIV in 2020. The Chiefs faced the San Francisco 49ers.

They traded touchdowns early on. Then San Francisco broke away. With seven minutes left in the game, KC was in trouble. They were behind 20-10. Facing third-and-15, the Chiefs needed something big. Patrick Mahomes launched a long bomb as he was being tackled. Down the field, Tyreek Hill broke free for the 44-yard catch.

Four plays later, KC scored a touchdown! Soon, they scored another to take the lead! Damien Williams ran 38 yards for another score, too! In six minutes, KC scored 21 unanswered! They earned a 31-20 victory and another Super Bowl ring!

Chapter 2

Chiefs All-Time Greats

QB Len Dawson led his team to the first Super Bowl. They returned for Super Bowl IV. Dawson and the Chiefs faced the Minnesota Vikings. Dawson set up running plays on a rainy, muddy field. Dawson took to the air in the fourth quarter. He threw a 41-yard pass to Otis Taylor. Touchdown! The Chiefs beat the Vikings, 23-7. Dawson was Super Bowl MVP. Now he's in the Hall of Fame!

Len Dawson

Bobby Bell posed for this silly picture!

Bobby Bell led the defense in that big game. Bell was feared by every quarterback. He set the NFL record for most **pick six** plays by a linebacker.

In the 1969 AFL Championship Game, Bell dominated the Jets. He tackled a runner inches from the goal line. The Chiefs won 13-6 to reach Super Bowl IV.

Cornerback Emmitt Thomas was another Chiefs defensive star. He holds the team record with 58 **interceptions**. During Super Bowl IV, Minnesota's QB went back to pass. Thomas reached out and pulled in the interception! KC won the Super Bowl!

Linebacker Willie Lanier had 27 interceptions. His biggest job was stopping running backs. He was a crushing tackler. Lanier was also a leader on the team. He inspired his teammates to keep getting better.

In 2008, the Chiefs retired Thomas' number.

Willie Lanier

For a long time, tight ends were mostly blockers. Players like Tony Gonzalez changed that. He was a basketball star in college. He was tall and very strong. For 12 seasons, he helped the Chiefs win. He even led the NFL in catches in 2004. Very few TEs have done that.

The best running backs in Chiefs history were Priest Holmes and Jamaal Charles. Holmes pounded out yards. He was very hard to tackle. Charles was speedy and quick. He is second all-time among running backs in a key stat. He averaged 5.4 yards per carry!

Tony Gonzalez

CHIEFS

RECORDS

These players piled up the best stats in Chiefs history. The numbers are career records through the 2019 season.

TOTAL TDs: Priest Holmes, 83

TD PASSES: Len Dawson, 237

PASSING YARDS: Len Dawson, 28,507

RECEIVING YARDS: Tony Gonzalez, 10,948

RUSHING YARDS: Jamaal Charles, 7,260

RECEPTIONS: Tony Gonzalez, 916

POINTS: Nick Lowery, 1,466

SACKS: Derrick Thomas, 126.5

Chapter 3
Chiefs Superstars

Patrick Mahomes began the 2017 season on the bench. He finished 2018 in the Pro Bowl! That year, he became the youngest player to throw 50 TDs in a season. He is the only QB to ever reach 5,000 passing yards and 50 TD passes in a season. No wonder he was the 2018 NFL MVP!

Mahomes finds ways to win. In a 2019 playoff game, the Chiefs were in trouble. They trailed Houston 24-0. Mahomes didn't panic. He threw four TDs in the second quarter—the Chiefs took the lead! They didn't stop scoring until they had won 51–31. The big comeback led to the Chiefs' Super Bowl win. Mahomes was named the Super Bowl MVP.

FUN FACT

Patrick Mahomes' dad, Pat, pitched 11 seasons in Major League Baseball.

Patrick Mahomes

Wide receiver Tyreek Hill may be the fastest player in the NFL. His nickname is "Cheetah"! Hill can outrun any defender. His speed helps him make lots of big plays. In the 2019 AFC title game, Hill's two touchdowns helped the Chiefs win.

Hill hauled in TD catches for 8 yards and 20 yards (above) to help Kansas City beat Tennessee 35–24 for the AFC title.

Tyreek Hill

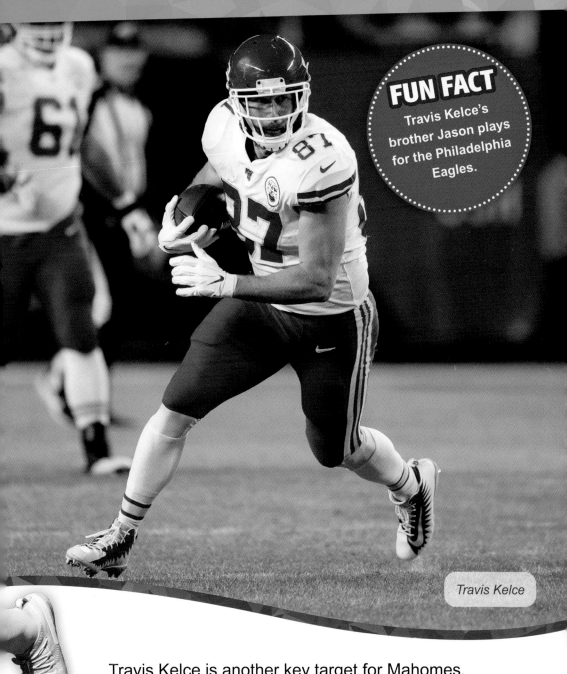

Travis Kelce

Travis Kelce is another key target for Mahomes. The big tight end has great hands. He is very hard to tackle. KC fans love his exciting plays! Kelce has topped 1,000 receiving yards four years in a row.

Damien Williams

Running back Damien Williams makes breaking tackles look easy. Defenders grab at him. Williams pushes for extra yards every time. In a key game against the Vikings, Williams burst through the line. He dodged defenders who fell at his feet. Williams ran 91 yards for a TD! KC won, 26-23!

Safety Tyrann Mathieu is the Chiefs' star defender. He can **shadow** any receiver. In a 2019 playoff game, Mathieu made a huge play. Houston aimed a pass downfield. It would have been a first down. Mathieu leaped and knocked away the pass! Houston punted, and never had the lead again.

With exciting offensive stars and a bruising defense, the Chiefs keep chopping away!

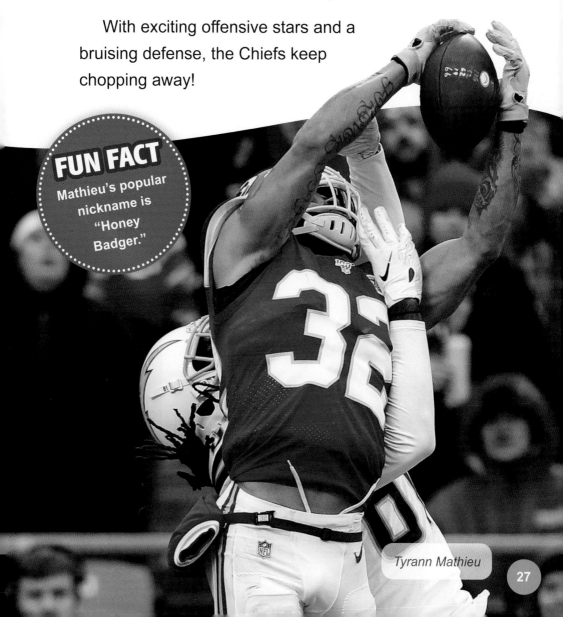

FUN FACT

Mathieu's popular nickname is "Honey Badger."

Tyrann Mathieu

THE BOOK

**After reading the book, it's time to think about what you learned.
Try the following exercises to jumpstart your ideas.**

RESEARCH

FIND OUT MORE. Where would you go to find out more about your favorite NFL teams and players? Check out NFL.com, of course. Each team also has its own website. What other sports information sites can you find? See if you can find other cool facts about your favorite team.

CREATE

GET ARTISTIC. Each NFL team has a logo. The Chiefs logo shows an arrowhead. Get some art materials and try designing your own Chiefs logo. Or create a new team and make a logo for it. What colors would you choose? How would you draw the mascot?

DISCOVER

GO DEEP! This books writes about how the Chiefs started in the American Football League. Read more about the AFL. What made it different from the NFL? What other teams moved from the AFL to the NFL? How would sports be different if the two leagues never came together?

GROW

GET OUT AND PLAY! You don't need to be in the NFL to enjoy football. You just need a football and some friends. Play touch or tag football. Or you can hang cloth flags from your belt; grab the belt and make the "tackle." See who has the best arm to be quarterback. Who is the best receiver? Who can run the fastest? Time to play football!

RESEARCH NINJA

Visit *www.ninjaresearcher.com/2336* to learn how
to take your research skills and book report writing to the next level!

RESEARCH ....

**DIGITAL
LITERACY
TOOLS**

SEARCH LIKE A PRO
Learn about how to use search
engines to find useful websites.

FACT OR FAKE?
Discover how you can tell
a trusted website from an
untrustworthy resource.

TEXT DETECTIVE
Explore how to zero in
on the information you
need most.

SHOW YOUR WORK
Research responsibly—
learn how to cite sources.

WRITE ....

GET TO THE POINT
Learn how to express your
main ideas.

PLAN OF ATTACK
Learn prewriting exercises
and create an outline.

**DOWNLOADABLE
REPORT
FORMS**

Further Resources

BOOKS

Coleman, Ted. *Patrick Mahomes.* North Mankato, Minn: North Star Editions, 2020.

Storm, Marysa. *Highlights of the Kansas City Chiefs.* Mankato, Minn.: Black Rabbit Books, 2019.

Whiting, Jim. *Kansas City Chiefs (The NFL Today).* Minneapolis: Creative Education, 2019.

WEBSITES

FACTSURFER

Factsurfer.com gives you a safe, fun way to find more information.

1. Go to www.factsurfer.com.

2. Enter "Kansas City Chiefs" into the search box and click 🔍

3. Select your book cover to see a list of related websites.

Glossary

bomb: a very long pass play. Mahomes threw a 60-yard bomb to Hill.

interception: a pass caught by the defense. Bell leaped up to make an interception of Joe Namath's pass.

pick six: an interception returned for a touchdown. Mathieu grabbed the interception and hit the end zone for a pick six.

rookie: a player in his first season of pro sports. Mahomes was a rookie in 2017.

shadow: when a player on defense stays very close to the opposing player. Mathieu used his speed to stay close to shadow A.J. Brown.

starting: describing a player who begins a game in his team's lineup. Mahomes went from backup to starting in 2018.

West Coast Offense: a style of play that uses lots of short passes. The Chiefs used the West Coast Offense to win lots of games.

Index

PHOTO CREDITS

About the Author

Mark and Solomon Shulman are a writing team with more than 150 books for young readers between them. They are based in New York City, yet they love no team more than the Buffalo Bills.